I'VE GOT A NEW JOB

By
Tim, Dan & Iulia Clarke
& Vez Roulston

Illustrated by **Anna Rolfe**

Introduction

Welcome to the *'I've Got a New Job'* pun book. It all started with four friends on a Peruvian adventure trekking the Inca Trail. To distract us from our aching joints, burning lungs and sweaty clothes we spent countless hours playing the travel game *'I've got a new job'*. We loved the puns so much we wrote them down and put them in a book (this one). We hope you enjoy them as much as we did!

Acknowledgments

Thank you to Anthony and Penny (Tim and Dan's parents) who put up with many hours of listening to our puns, whilst also trekking up mountains with us. They contributed a few too. Thank you to Super Dario, our Inca Trail guide, for tolerating our puns and keeping us alive. Thank you to our friends who humoured us and suggested new puns; particularly the Pagets, Lyalls, Lattimers and Halls, and those we possibly have forgotten. Finally we're hugely grateful to Anna, our illustrator, and to Sujo and Kiet for editing and formatting this book.

I've got a new job

What is it?

I'm a midwife

How's it going?

I'm expecting a lot

I've got a new job

What is it?

I'm an astronaut

How's it going?

It's out of this world

I've got a new job

What is it?

I'm a bin man

How's it going?

Rubbish

I've got a new job

What is it?

I've become a chemist

How's it going?

I'm in my element

I've got a new job

What is it?

I repair sinks

How's it going?

Draining

I've got a new job

What is it?

I sell walking boots

How's it going?

Sole destroying

I've got a new job

What is it?

I work with dyslexic boxers

How's it going?

O.K.

I've got a new job

What is it?

I install children's play areas

How's it going?

Swings and roundabouts

I've got a new job

What is it?

I work in a magnet factory

How's it going?

I feel I am being pulled in the wrong direction

I've got a new job

What is it?

I'm a doctor

How's it going?

Pretty sick

I've got a new job

What is it?

I am a human scarecrow

How's it going?

I've been told I'm outstanding
in my field

I've got a new job

What is it?

I'm a chiropractor

How's it going?

It's hard to not feel manipulated

I've got a new job

What is it?

I make mirrors

How's it going?

I can see myself enjoying it

I've got a new job

What is it?

I produce anti-dandruff shampoo

How's it going?

It's a bit flaky

I've got a new job

What is it?

I make batteries

How's it going?

It has its positives and negatives

I've got a new job

What is it?

I charge people for crossing bridges

How's it going?

It's toll-erable

I've got a new job

What is it?

I manufacture hot water bottles

How's it going?

I'm warming to it

I've got a new job

What is it?

I work in earthquake relief

How's it going?

Pretty shaky

I've got a new job

What is it?

I'm a mechanic

How's it going?

Exhausting

I've got a new job

What is it?

I sell arm bands

How's it going?

Keeps my head above the water

ARM BANDS
SMALL – £2.50
MED – £2.50
LARGE – £2.50

I've got a new job

What is it?

I work at a sausage factory

How's it going?

It is the wurst job I've ever had

I've got a new job

What is it?

I'm a piano teacher

How's it going?

It's not my forte

I've got a new job

What is it?

I work as a school teacher

How's it going?

Class

I've got a new job

What is it?

I work at a bird sanctuary

How's it going?

It pays the bills

I've got a new job

What is it?

I repair pottery

How's it going?

It's not all it's cracked up to be

I've got a new job

What is it?

I work in a creperie

How's it going?

Flipping amazing

I've got a new job

What is it?

I am a triple jump athlete

How's it going?

I'm coming on leaps and bounds

I've got a new job

What is it?

I've started working at a butchers

How's it going?

I'm making a right pig's ear of it

I've got a new job

What is it?

I help maintain river populations

How's it going?

Pretty mainstream

I've got a new job

What is it?

I produce naked calendars

How's it going?

It's very revealing

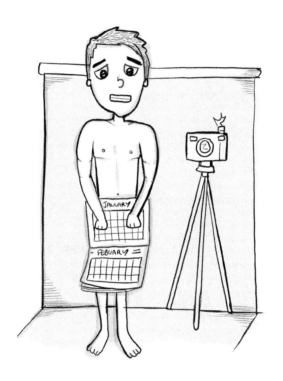

I've got a new job

What is it?

I produce rubber bands

How's it going?

Stretching me to the limit

I've got a new job

What is it?

I deliver mail

How's it going?

I'll keep you posted

I've got a new job

What is it?

I build bridges

How's it going?

Not good, but I'll get over it

I've got a new job

What is it?

I sell parasols

How's it going?

It's pretty shady

I've got a new job

What is it?

I work in a hardware store

How's it going?

I'm nailing it

I've got a new job

What is it?

I've become a forest ranger

How's it going?

Treemendous

I've got a new job

What is it?

I work at a polling station

How's it going?

Ticks all the boxes

I've got a new job

What is it?

I've become a farmer

How's it going?

It's growing on me

I've got a new job

What is it?

I work in a slaughter house

How's it going?

I'm making a killing

I've got a new job

What is it?

I work in a Mojito bar

How's it going?

Mint

I've got a new job

What is it?

I've become a rower

How's it going?

Oarsome

I've got a new job

What is it?

I work on the underground

How's it going?

It's a bit beneath me

I've got a new job

What is it?

I work for a boiler company

How's it going?

Not great. I can't take the pressure

I've got a new job

What is it?

I work in an ice cream van

How's it going?

Fab

I've got a new job

What is it?

I'm a waiter

How's it going?

Tip top

I've got a new job

What is it?

I work on an owl reserve

How's it going?

It's a hoot

I've got a new job

What is it?

I'm conserving panda habitats

How's it going?

Bamboozling

I've got a new job

What is it?

I fix car windscreens

How's it going?

Shattering at times

I've got a new job

What is it?

I work for the Red Cross

How's it going?

It's a relief

I've got a new job

What is it?

I supply helium in bulk

How's it going?

It's a barrel of laughs

I've got a new job

What is it?

_____

How's it going?

_____

Please send us some of your own at –
ivegotanewjob@hotmail.com

Printed in Great Britain
by Amazon